A Home in the Wilderness

by Morgan Lloyd

illustrated by Burgandy Beam

Editorial Offices: Glenview, Illinois • Parsippany, New Jersey • New York, New York
Sales Offices: Needham, Massachusetts • Duluth, Georgia • Glenview, Illinois
Coppell, Texas • Ontario, California • Mesa, Arizona

Every effort has been made to secure permission and provide appropriate credit for photographic material. The publisher deeply regrets any omission and pledges to correct errors called to its attention in subsequent editions.

Unless otherwise acknowledged, all photographs are the property of Scott Foresman, a division of Pearson Education.

Photo locators denoted as follows: Top (T), Center (C), Bottom (B), Left (L), Right (R), Background (Bkgd)

Illustrations by Burgandy Beam

Photograph 16 Corbis

ISBN: 0-328-13240-3

5 6 7 8 9 10 V010 14 13 12 11 10 09 08 07

"Whoa!" Papa called. The horse and wagon came to a stop.

"This is our homestead," he said. "What do you think?"

Jeremiah and Ruthie looked around. The prairie stretched as far as they could see. It looked like a sea of grass.

"It's a good place for our new home," Mama said.

They had left the east to start a new life. Jeremiah remembered what Papa had said: "Free people need land to live on, and there is free land out west." They had filled a wagon with the things that they would need to make a new home in the wilderness. They had pots and pans, tools, quilts, and a little black stove. Most of the wagon was filled with food: flour, dried fruit, bacon, and seeds for planting. They had even brought four chickens.

That first night was warm and tranquil. Mama made rabbit stew, and they sat around the fire talking. The stars were bright. Back east, you could hardly see the stars, but here, it seemed as though you could see the whole galaxy.

"It will not be easy to farm this land and make it our home," Papa said. "But if we live on it for five years, the land will be ours. We will work hard. And we will always remember how good it is to be free."

At first they slept outside. Late one night, after the Moon had come up, Jeremiah heard a coyote howling in the distance. He was scared, but Papa was right next to him. He pulled the quilt closer. He would be glad when they had a house with walls!

Mama, Papa, Ruthie, and Jeremiah were very busy. It seemed that there was always more work to be done. They dug a well for water. Papa taught Jeremiah how to cut sod for the roof. It was hard work. Jeremiah's hands and back hurt.

Ruthie helped Mama build a coop for the chickens and plant a vegetable garden. They planted potatoes, squash, beans, and watermelons. Later, they plowed the land in order to plant corn.

Slowly, the little plot of land began to feel like home. One afternoon, Jeremiah and Ruthie were out exploring. Jeremiah loved to sit in the tall grass and watch for birds or other wildlife. Suddenly, Ruthie grabbed Jeremiah's hand.

"Jeremiah, look!" she shouted.

Jeremiah looked up and saw a dark, twisting cloud coming towards them. It was a tornado! The two raced home.

"Mama! Papa!" they yelled. "There's a twister coming!"

Jeremiah and Ruthie sat with Mama and Papa inside the little sod house. They could hear the rumbling sound of the wind outside. Minutes passed, and then it was quiet.

They stepped outside to see what had happened. The roof had been badly damaged. Much of the corn lay broken on the ground. Worst of all, the chickens were gone. Ruthie began to cry.

"We are lucky to be safe," Mama said.

Many of the vegetables in the garden were small, so they had not been hurt by the tornado. The family fixed what they could. Weeks went by and the crops grew. Then came a week of rain.

"A little rain will do the crops good," Mama said, trying to smile.

But it was more than a little rain. Soon the roof began to leak. Water dripped in. Clumps of mud began to fall on everything. They even fell on Ruthie.

At last the rain ended. The vegetables in the garden grew ripe from the sun. Soon the corn was ready to harvest. Ruthie and Jeremiah worked hard. They helped pick vegetables from the garden. It was good to have so much food. Jeremiah knew they would need it for the winter.

When winter came, the family stayed inside. Mama and Ruthie worked on a quilt. At night, Papa would play music on his banjo and they would sing.

All winter the wind blew hard and cold. Papa would go hunting. Sometimes he caught a rabbit, but other times there was no meat.

One morning Ruthie did not get up. Mama felt her forehead. "Ruthie has a fever," she said.

Ruthie stayed in bed all day. She did not eat. Jeremiah brought her water and covered her with an extra quilt.

Days passed and Ruthie did not get better. The weather got even worse. It snowed so hard that it got dark outside. Papa brought the horse into the house so it would not freeze to death. By the second day, snow covered the windows and they could not see out. Mama melted snow on the stove for water. They were running out of food.

On the fourth morning, Jeremiah woke up and felt sunlight on his face.

"Ruthie, wake up!" he shouted. "It's stopped snowing!"

Eventually the weather began to get warmer, and Ruthie started to feel well. She ate more and soon she could walk around.

One day Jeremiah and Papa were out walking past the corn fields. Suddenly, a bird shot up in the air in front of them.

"A prairie chicken!" said Papa. The bird landed again not far from them. "See?" Papa pointed down through the grass. Jeremiah saw a nest of grass lined with feathers. The nest was full of eggs.

Papa took off his hat and they filled it with grass. They gently put the eggs in the hat, one by one.

"We can bring them to Ruthie," Jeremiah said, "and she can have chickens again."

As they walked back home, Jeremiah thought about their first year on the homestead. They had lived through many challenges. Their new life was not easy, but Jeremiah knew that together they would make it great.

Life in the Wild

This story is set in Nebraska in the 1870s. Many African Americans joined the thousands of homesteaders who moved west in those years.

The homesteaders faced many challenges. Weather on the plains was harsh. The settlers experienced tornadoes, drought, dust storms, prairie fires, thunderstorms, hail, blizzards, and cold.

They hunted wild animals for food, but animals could also be a threat. Some wild animals damaged crops or hurt livestock. Living alone was perhaps the hardest of all. Neighbors, doctors, and help were far away.